Internal Rhyme

Also by Scott Thurston

Poems Nov 89 – Jun 91 (Writers Forum, London, 1991)
State(s) walk(s) (Writers Forum, London, 1994)
Fragments (The Lilliput Press, Norwich, 1994)
Sleight of Foot (with Miles Champion, Helen Kidd and Harriet Tarlo)
                   (Reality Street Editions, London, 1996)
Two Sequences (RWC, Sutton, 1998)
Turns (with Robert Sheppard)
                   (Ship of Fools/Radiator, Liverpool, 2003)
Of Utility (Spanner, Hereford, 2005)
Hold (Shearsman Books, Exeter, 2006)
Momentum (Shearsman Books, Exeter, 2008)

SCOTT THURSTON

Internal Rhyme

Shearsman Books
Exeter

Published in the United Kingdom in 2010 by
Shearsman Books Ltd
58 Velwell Road
Exeter EX4 4LD

ISBN 978-1-84861-090-3
First Edition

Acknowledgements

Some of these poems have previously appeared in the following magazines
and anthologies: *Axolotl, crtl+alt+del, Damn the Caesars, if P then Q,
Liverpool Poets* (Erbacce, 2008)*, Penumbra, Shearsman, Text 2* (Bury
Council, 2009), *Veer Away*. Many thanks to the editors.

Special thanks are due to James Davies for publishing the
opening seven poems as *Matchbox* 9 and to Simon Taylor
for his accompanying photographs therein.

Contents

I

internal rhyme

I can feel your

eternal flask

of relief at the end of

pleasure you can't

stand at the gateway

possible dynamic

you will terribly

a species of adder magic

badge by my side

leave out those signs

withdrawal symptoms

measure the hybrids

the larger logic that makes

critical constructions

well un-read

in visibility give me

totality the weight of

my feet in a new way

ignites a prospect of

ground to other

fiery remote surgery

an encased circuit

never refusing

the whole without

me dropping down moving

full flow force field

balance relation to

this searing contact

perfect platinum breaks

of touch without

suppressing difference

death my enemy

ever the face crags

the young argue

to finitude open

let's stay closer than

the pay off of ages

for themselves consigned

essentially mortal

well for pure water

form an invitation to

radical plurality

take my hand

mathematics of waves

disappear in different

disjunctive others

lovely wolf-skull

how to find us

on this train can

smoke expand upon

death coming fast

if there is a driver

they make themselves known

a limit plane we heard

but got out of the way

in time the open

sacred tomb bewilders

strong palettes death as

end constantly

secret is scared is

a wonder tense of

punctuation without

being against itself

is it only an argument of style, absolute fear of
the scale that establishes real measures? I risk
my attenuated trunk the crown so far from the
root thinkable only without opposition

a slip on shifting interposed surfaces
creation of a sharp drop in dignity lost face
bounces a patch to snap back in time
an inexplicable forfeit horrific unaccountability

how to live without

me over and over

denial if you don't

prey you are not

moving to recoup

a reversal but a

motion carries right

by stretching time

god innocent death kills

little by little a total

dance springing on

a dancer

a grazed recall not

tolerance of particles

out of the system

making life visible

for James Powell

virtuous knowledge

practice evidence and

a real return showing

who knows the most

quick and dirty look

to blank page whole

essence of systems

in turn left only

sharing creativity is best

reason new without blame

engagement transfers

unthinkable images

to bear back

through thinking the

co-creation stays always

more than a title

about this boy what
nerves behind this
blind longing welded to
a mask of class

transpires to be slick
rhetoric starts to expose
strength case hardened
beguiling intellect

a tempting torture
straight where your
will you have been
it is that

to explain sell it to me
pattern breaks when
able to judge what
you have lost

me and my shadow

restlessly how to love

if things are hidden

when it is sought

turning relentlessly

without god it's lost

running out of time

ought it to be given

under force of

spanning blame to a

recuperative love

at the end

circumstance? Purports

drafted report numbing

notes of the sad songs

of the celebration

I said too much

adequate to my head

there is no difference

there is pure multiple

slow down moving leaves

at the top of the trees

between difference and identity

there is there is

vicious penetration

internal enigma

hidden on display

the power

folding into torsion

unjust pain untried

provides a measure for

the movement and the rest

a conservative impulse

lodges bakes a thin

rough escarpment traps

taste a trellis stapled on

tacky postcard view

fortunes ruined chambers

kinds of infinity

lay waste to wilds

tracks down former

run into me down

to sullen swerve of

the deep

laid waste to submerged

shredded nullity what

stalks into cells

within me

at this rate of change

snatching options as they

back from the overall

favours of esteem or

to real time composition

instead of wrapping back

live it out first then

by then actually start

I buffet forth and back

occur rather than working

plan it does me no

charity is a commitment

a kind of blunt lie

a shape onto myself

write it not too late

whilst on the way

I thee obdurate implacable

this spectacle sunk into

bring it up on the plinth

a triumph of sudden

your broken spear demands

a stage managed sulk

shattered attention tries

unfeeling grace of servitude

your longing detractors

exile anonymous indulgence

beneath sky lights lots

distend or do they

gift you the feelings of

lying in a sad heap

of clouded ranges distract

uplift, mend, suspend?

I can't survive it   this priceless uniqueness

borne down on me   for your attention

in the archive   you simply suppose it

in gratitude   for the lexicon

not to beg a   perpetually recuperated

loss hard-won   but to launch the

implosion of negativity   the strict statute

bearer standard   of our ends

where it is that simple

expression tied into

a cake-walk

to a pleasing

a process of difficult

lines as economic support

a frog-march

dead-end blankness

what one alters here

when all one wants is

to sustain

a note melting

gets undone here again

to make a mark

some untoward feeling

into brevity

no fear loves me

I accept a feint

rock in it draw a

line up the lie

where I cannot force

to the familiar – put a

sword by my side

to the hilt

trouble is brewing

space clear air

tolerance fears

welcomed back

welcome it to fresh

still torrents sustained

inflicted by youth

at the new bazaar

a wren upon a board
give it to me hard
status through a ruse
to straiten a muse

that shot potential stir
a reason to infer
a cunning temper lies
behind corrupt prosody

whack a fly on a bin
away so forcefully it
doubles in intensity
your innovative ego

what you have thrown
back to you returns
your surface only burns
to forestall revolution

constantly preying at

contracts sends us

a tension useless once

something happened

a boundary which suddenly

scattering all seeking

acquired simply to mark

we threw stones at

something till we got

scared until we were

there are no longer

hold us control us

scared because we were

scared no longer that

any sites can

even love us

I can't write about   what I did what

I gave to whom I   gave it where it

took place at what   time who gave it

what was intended   what was felt

if it was a transaction   of sorts the modality

involved inflected   upon if it could

have been considered   a test of sorts

if any chance of   belief forgot

that she would   rotate in an isolated

square at night   parade through

ventilation dance   without movement

crafted intolerable   little trainers

I'm smashed in   educated lack

shut out as if by   caste of mind down

a fallen crest   to actual parallel

run way or concentric   or the same not the same

II

turning to leave   through a door

having fought our   presence I bolt

unnoticed commitment   unresisted course

to danger   given up altogether

on some other flight   the invisible worm

is time where in   dread to fall I

stand not fast   finally impersonal

style is entirely   inescapably yours

where flowering reeds   grow in profusion

dark actions differ   select or combine

in love an answer   to death being

spoken across   a dish of irises

my hidden friend   were you stolen

kept on display   in the museum

what you say   hears my listening

wax on a ground   creates relief

I have grown into   an institution the choice of

a coat grants anew   membership identifies stratum

feeling of gained weight   of authority scared to death

in a poem interrupted   by senior figures

inspired by an ethics   of movement turn towards

in public space in   time or away from

articulate gesture   occasionally a decision

to simply not meet   accepting difference

an injunction to stay   safe as if I was

already as if it were   desirable or even

possible this necessity   to err on the side

of caution to court   a taut cauterization

I think if there

ought not to be

a civilisation

should try to

love the lock with

measuring accurately

to cut through the

spray renovating

are mysteries they

begotten here that

can end is clear that it

preserve itself is not

sensitive detection

allowing a quiet line

commotion like a sharp

the poor land

what I give myself to   haunted by surface

a polished shine   or cloudy patina

it takes art to maintain   a perpetual crisis

taking everything   you have

I want to give   my heart out

to your ideal world   in its tension

I have to wait   for the memory

for the poem   to make it right

I touch something new
the west gentle tremor
already granted to
compound how you set

control under your hand
a spectacle to resist
your very substance
untoward uncalmed

again red smudge in
how to achieve visibility
independent form of
it to run from your

sensational movement
by branded intelligence
very tasty in harm
senses of heredity

to be on the trail of   several answers

is not a question   what I wasn't looking for

is here   view across a city

that you never   visited where I work

again in the company of   a famous critic

choosing the show   over a talk what is

lost here only   cleaved to a source of

the next bent   twisting point

rain falls what
washing off residue
they collect below
they concentrate

clarity is that
of ideologies as
in a system do
your troubles

exercise escalate
to me it is all the
priorities deterred
through conduits

it is all the same
same to you lost
the dialogues run
to the sea

I thought I was going   to die today I felt

so good, tense   perfect in this monochrome

culture I build   self in this space

give responsibility   changing the situation

where the bounds are   already blown irrevocably

pieces I must pick up   taking too much on

I am already spoken for   in this moonlight

I am not my own   loan myself only

after Badiou

what happens versus	what is on the edge
the void a halting	point encounters something
no longer itself reflection	on revolution is an element
of revolution chance	fragment wrested from inclusion
pure advent meaning	it always escapes what happens
versus what happens	in thought is truth what
comes to being or what	unfolds being nothing but
multiplicity turns in	eternal movement

when did you see

extraordinary pressure

expression is movement

in need of urgency

immaculately dressed

important culture

like the moon

changes, decays

sight in parataxis under

notion whose best

knowledge can't be had

you have too much time

for the office self

in full flight passes

revives silence

returns always

such a way   in which everything
uttered becomes   poetry resistant to
the materials   resistance of the
materials in time   endlessly changing

moon through clouds   affects progress as
cloud affects warming sun affects cooling
everything you write will disappear soon
take trouble to mend a structure on the way

the road to ennui   easy take a left or

a right turn and   you're there rising sea

level growth in heat   how long to keep

emptying out knowledge   information till it stales

I don't doubt that   I can't keep this

new solar system   closed circling cells

diverse planetary matters   following transverse traces

disappearing this time   into a new universe

replacing my licence   document after 17 years

signature counter   signature anxiety

a maquette graph of   outlines registering

stress peaks   of internal rhyme

a famous artist   at the next table

adopts his text   recollects himself

in constant remaking   his mark over and over

retrospective gift   of document 17 years earlier

that community is   a process over time

what you desire   to protect what demands

you stay still   you are necessary

in your voice   you are missed

I want readiness   to give my gentle

ego over determined   life over life

into history for all   time honed over

generations   redetermined

after Badiou

suppose all	language can be
inscribed in	the unity of an expression
undecidable lost	grip surges forth
it took place	it was given
nothing governs it	pure choice
which door	no gap
almost nothing	almost everything
we know of truth	is only knowledge

not a block but

emotional information

dim intensity

makes possible

a crocus in snow

I have to hold

takes me up

though lips constrain

slowing down

too dense to process

what the technology

lethally intervenes in

that I can't control

it boils in me

a threat entreats

a sullen heat

something dim   ignited in me

in relation to   a strained guard

endless desire   canalised again

contracted point   breaks forth

give me a beat   over tones of

articulatory effort   bodies washed up

on the beach   standards of

international service   blinds shutters

what have you   passed me on to

this caged bird   sings and talks

needs contact   admits limitation

tense stimulation   provokes growth

your telling tale   turn and spin

cannot articulate   relations of difference

I can't critique   suffer anxiety

your planted lets   turn right out in me

III

adder in the spine

in you in me

from the earth

from the sky

cross a truth

from the heart

truth is always

using awareness

dances differently

what is taken up

what is taken down

having taken place

along one's path

from the sex

already present

making choices

a white hare   flashes down a cliff

we enter the moor   finding a gully

lose the horizon   following a river

in the mist   to its downfall

its flow held mid-air   by the wind and

blown back up the   rock as we descend

jacob's ladder the   same thought occurs

moving up   the moving down

I'm hearing shadow

so violently

without empathy

my excess cruelty

where I meet you

thinking you

turns back on me

with impunity

holding to what

visible desire

only me in

that not shadow

cannot be completed

embarrasses not

the dance judging

but shatter yourself

sometimes you

sometimes you

trust accidentally

dead love

the commons

reverse private

the smarter

grab power

arrive home

don't text me

I am not

leaving

being enclosed

and public

the dumber

use it

a second mouth opens in the corner

of the first says something

different to what permitted by its

partner means opposition

or not attempt a traverse into

sustainability insatiability beckons

from a sideline slip inside a bit to

bring it formally out throw it off

today again   resistance to the

music play   patcher shut out

of the ceremony   taking the early

cues emblems of   disagreement

on no noon   look upon me

looking upon it   visible covering

the invisible   I go out of sight

holding back   at the crossing

what has shot   the system of

balance integrity   myth tested

against itself   does ingenuity

traverse time   remain creative

exhaust technique   pass through

its moment into   current relics

doubt reflected   back to itself

to account for   positive capability

a studied counsel   of self and co

perpetuated need   roughly out on

the thin edge of   the wedge

looking always to   drive it deeper

subject a hole   in knowledge

virtual recollection   the universal is

always incalculable   sudden emergence

deactivating all   describable structures

a plane quietly

hoves into view

benevolent as if

there belying

brightly lit

in a grey dusk

it has always been

the inevitable

where it is

looking for her

if they can do it

singing at dawn

I am not

among her friends

so can I

live over again

fully inhabit

the more you

hold grips

the living

all the masks

resist the more

the dead support

energy flows

from reader

when sustained

their position

imposed upon

to writer

by acceptance of

not being

set free

imagine those touch able representations of

the visual over standing under

strength language creates mutual knowledge

double edged swords

beside the scholar's rock chrysanthemum

blooms a toad patiently waits

watches ants moving deliberately

deconstructing a butterfly

moving fast   slow at the same

time risking   improvisation

again familiar   game terminal

attention span   encouragement

your fit of   uncommon lucidity

implacable logic   leads us somewhere

strange forbidden   reconfigured

passing through   your isolation

I put my hands up
what it doesn't know
taught me that I
have some other

spy on the moon
it hasn't yet
forgot everything
mind inside

when I wants it
a narrow gauge
trains the approach
builds up a steam

goes looking along
railway beware of
requiring a halt
to connect with a loop

when I magnify   you magnify me

precisely to tolerate   the space between

a double sun   converging solar

plexus accepts what   energy offers

I could give it   to you around

but not about   is a cross and

beyond light   flees to infinity

finishes the world   in revelation

You have us   at a disadvantage

beauty conceives   its own shape

lets no-one intervene   innocent

in its desire not to be   innocence

this emotional   structure, pattern

set of relationships   is real needs

to be seen   understood

to inform action   fight for joy

after Klimt

Nuda Veritas   holds up a mirror

hands that draw   me in to see

is it bad to   please the many

be carried along   when life is a struggle

the painter creates his own society

and banks the cash   looks at the private

centring the public hatred of the eternal

turns away   from interior view

are we so   scared of infinity

we need to   traverse it

not transcend it   we can't transcend it

when desires   presence is absent

absences desire is   present as

the right to be   acknowledged as

the witness to   your own self

dance as if life   depended on it

small wren is

realizing humility

to achieve art

rational and honest

beautiful activity

tempered cunning

with economical

use of others

don't become invisible

or exploit others

examine yourself

use your wit

as a form of defence

work to win status

little king

your native discipline

A Summer for Cy Twombly

sigh signs   his way into

my heart   making it look

like it wasn't   made this

breath is not   a passage

infinite and yet   so brief this

love affair lasts   no time at all

the lovers encounter   pure difference

to overcome it   beneath the waves

noticing that   someone wants

something energetic   company sex

realigns angles   of relation

mirror reflects   back construction

something undecidable   decided

declaring valence   where there was nothing

a real undergoing   change fixing

the present   as it disappears

IV

little boats bright   colours against dark

waters a cross   shaped mast lines

buoyed to mooring   across from a boat

which stays   under the surface

when my loss has   made it back to

you in time to   show it you

appear to disappear   over and over

in stability   in the medium

something for all

inaugurate

in favour of

negating

time acts to

change decision

truth versus

the universal

love the many

the same

in the rain

without end

ways of being

infinite

our rights

in completeness

one minute I'm

stuck polarity

shocks into sense

projected anew

the next I'm

foreign to myself

not produced

by restaging

losing hold across

an act of violence

distorted feeling

occasion for change

winning thought

identical to something

shapes itself

its past

broke a vow   to myself and

broke it back   vision without

tradition tradition   without vision

loving the distant   state at a distance

release reset   being despite

death fear of   the collective

tactile attack   signature gesture

the trifle termed   mortality

commit to a

false hope in

philosophy starts

out in crowds

crime of arousing

stricken sound

a sudden shut

climbs down

a slim incision

the heart lifted

bloodless just

discovered

across the chest

clean out

another toy

in a dream

fear is not   a gift given

easily taken in   to a tumult

a cutting   of red rock

passes through   blown out dunes

from the triassic   that which cleaves

to a ledge   for survival

a temporary envelope   of opportunity

about to collapse   might make it

orphan letter gives   a clue to

what to think   make and do

struck bending   one world regime

into another   more unreachable

flaming chariot   collides with

another thought in   the turn of

the body   remaking the

visible, thinkable   possible

if it's true   that another world

pulls at this one   should we walk

the ecotone   what gain we

from it only   knowledge

higgs boson   switching point of

transcendental   empiricism

we must surely   gain and lose

all this time   over again

recognition a wave

across difference

write humanity

a hand writing

across a courtyard

connects us

in a larger script

on the wall

a simple gesture

ideal friendship

respect, acceptance

autumn leaves

contains in it

understanding

equality

under our feet

you don't have to   defend every decision

lodged in place   would you disavow

it the hand that   mocked them and

the heart that fed   stamped on lifeless

act of thought   face to face

energy faces off   softening in reaction to

hardness thought of   act addressed to

whom does direct   address address?

how precious	individuation

knowing when	to emerge when

to remain	hidden

stopping	the dream

to prevent	a crime

fox diplomacy	kenning over

conning you	to love

your creativity	too much

lost object still   lodged in

my sternum its loss   always part

of its history   from the start it's

only gone   not lost

link the poetic   traces inscribed

directly in reality   with the artificial

assembly of complex   machines for

understanding   polytopia

what is a toy   faces a unique

configuration in   time transparent

levels of universe   layers of marks

maps, guides   accounts of journeys

why should this be   any more or any

less perfect than any   thing else

circular form   punctuated

by incident necessary   for survival

                    .

attention in   a tension

of utility   o futility

bound together   in speech

work makes free   time visible

in sensible matter   thought over again

act or acted   upon overcome

by will asserts   making is seeing

seeing is making   saying over again

in a time

dawn a pattern

shows its own

calm world

before a solstice

of electric lamps

implacable logic

all in order

necessary light

of stratocumulus

will shed light on

holding a candle

boiling at the edge

will disrupt this

questionable motive

rising sun

a double kiss received in memory

ecology and landscape development have

your eyes closed aspects of a world

fallen into place inside a head

highly personal in impersonal terms

a real tense sense of menace

to see one's life as a general manifestation or

an individual one independent experiences

consciousness proceeds beyond itself

acknowledging my fellow human in the park

speak beyond myself red sun on horizon

despair at loss of freedom the responsibility taken

looking up at bare
infinity apparent
to distinguish finite
from infinitely plural

branch makes
a task emerging
mortal existence
being forever

but why pay
subtle energy
world? egotistical
psyche's open

attention to dreams
to live in this
fantasy versus
boundless imagination

approaching an end

to sum up

better to attend

but found wanting

no short history

the state capital

original innovative

regenerate

fighting urge

at height

to what's underfoot

to look back

to brutality

vicious as ever no

lies to replace

the old

Blake's God   infinite in all things

Newton seeing only   himself in formulas

maths as violence   rather than absolute

truth risking   desire for absolute

cleared space   nostalgia for escape

fantasies   zero divided by

zero infinite or   what gives

form   to nothingness

after all   death is only

ever always   beginning over

again this   terrifying integrity of

joy   excessive innovation

you found   your own company

shared language   relying on presence

still telling   what is told

in completion   in finitude

www.ingramcontent.com/pod-product-compliance
Lightning Source LLC
Chambersburg PA
CBHW022201080426
42734CB00006B/528